Canadian Commu

Don Massey

Contents

Three Canadian Communities: Where Are They?

ARCTIC OCEAN

UNITED STATES

YUKON

NORTHWEST TERRITORIES

NUNAVUT

CANADA

BRITISH COLUMBIA

SASKATCHEWAN

ALBERTA

MANITOBA

PACIFIC OCEAN

Regina

N
W   E
S

UNITED STATES

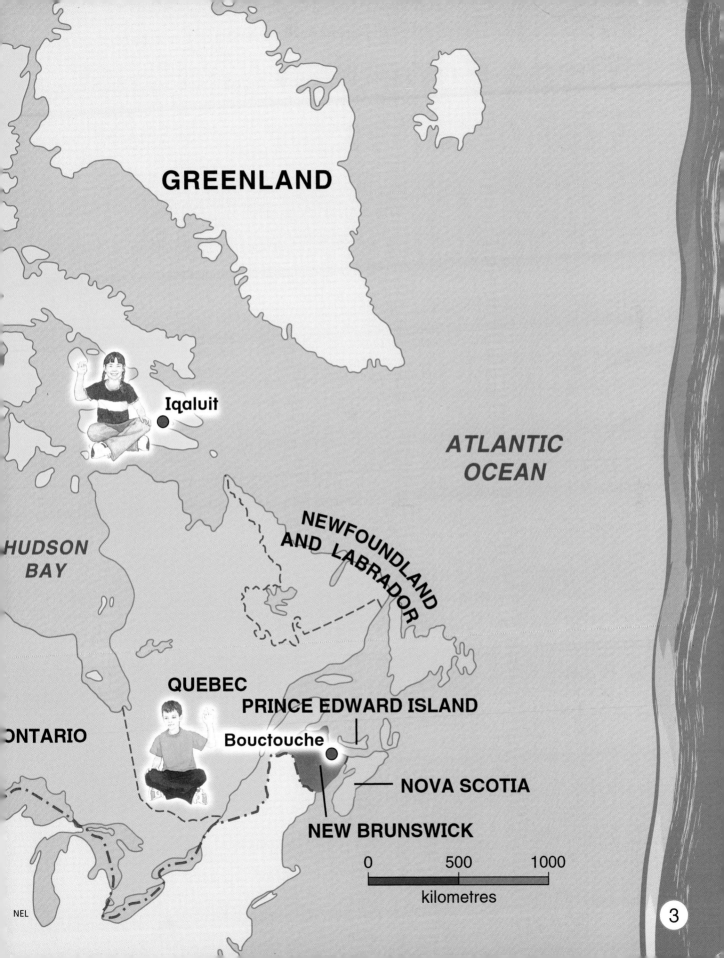

GREENLAND

ATLANTIC
OCEAN

Iqaluit

HUDSON
BAY

NEWFOUNDLAND
AND LABRADOR

QUEBEC

PRINCE EDWARD ISLAND

ONTARIO

Bouctouche

NOVA SCOTIA

NEW BRUNSWICK

0   500   1000

kilometres

NEL

Three Canadian Citizens: Welcome!

A citizen is someone who is part of a community. Let's meet three Canadian citizens.

Welcome! My name is Linda. This is a picture of my city, Regina. It is the capital of my province, Saskatchewan. We are in Western Canada. We are part of the Prairies.

Tunngasugit! My name is Meeka. This picture shows Iqaluit, the small city where I live. It is the capital of my territory, Nunavut. We are on the coast of Baffin Island in Northern Canada. We are an Inuit community.

Bienvenue! My name is Michel. Here is a picture of my town, Bouctouche. It is in the province of New Brunswick. We are on the East Coast of Canada. We are part of l'Acadie, or Acadia.

1. **If you could talk to these three children about where you live, what would you tell them?**

2. **What is being a citizen all about?**

Our Physical Geography

One way to describe a community is to talk about its land, water, and climate. This is called physical geography. Canada is a big country and has many different regions, such as Prairie, Arctic, and coastal. Linda, Meeka, and Michel tell us about their regions.

Land

I live on the Prairies, which is flat land like in this picture. Prairie soil is good for farming. I like our big skies and the way the fields seem to go on forever.

I live in the Arctic, on a coast. Our land is rocky and hilly with no trees. I like the mountains, which are not too far from us. This picture shows plants on the tundra in summer. Tundra is treeless, frozen ground that has a top layer of thawed soil in summer.

I live on a coast near the ocean. Our land is sandy and marshy with good farmland near us. We have a long sand dune called La Dune de Bouctouche. Here is a picture of it. The dune stretches out into the ocean, and my family likes to walk along it.

What could you tell someone about the land around your community?

Bodies of Water

Most communities are near bodies of water. Bodies of water are types of water, such as oceans, lakes, bays, inlets, rivers, streams, and creeks. What will Linda, Meeka, and Michel tell us?

Regina is far from a big body of water like an ocean. Wascana Creek runs through the city, but it is small. The Qu'Appelle River is near us. Communities need a large water supply, so we built Wascana Lake right in the city. This is a picture of it.

Iqaluit is near the Arctic Ocean. We are on Koojesse Inlet, which is part of Frobisher Bay. This is a picture of the Sylvia Grinnell River, which runs through our city. There are also many lakes and streams near us.

Bouctouche is near the Atlantic Ocean. We are on Bouctouche Bay. The Bouctouche River runs through the town. This picture shows the river. We also have many streams around us.

Regina's Bodies of Water

Iqaluit's Bodies of Water

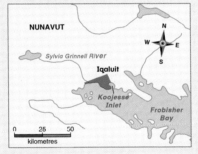

Bouctouche's Bodies of Water

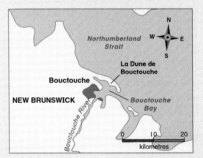

What are the main bodies of water in or near your community?

Climate

Climate means what a region's weather is usually like. Let's see what these reports say about the climates of Regina, Iqaluit, and Bouctouche.

Regina: My Climate Report

Season	Average Temperature (how hot or cold it usually is)	Average Precipitation (the usual amount of snow and rain)
Winter (January)	−16°C	15 millimetres
Spring (April)	5°C	24 millimetres
Summer (July)	19°C	65 millimetres
Fall (October)	5°C	22 millimetres

Notes:
What I like most about our climate is the sunshine. We get more sunshine than any other capital city in Canada. Sometimes it is very windy, and we get big thunderstorms in the summer. I like to watch the clouds and the changes in our big Prairie sky.

Iqaluit: My Climate Report

Season	Average Temperature (how hot or cold it usually is)	Average Precipitation (the usual amount of snow and rain)
Winter (January)	−26°C	21 millimetres
Spring (April)	−15°C	28 millimetres
Summer (July)	8°C	59 millimetres
Fall (October)	−5°C	37 millimetres

Notes:
I like that our Arctic climate is different from other climates in Canada. On winter days we have a few hours of sunlight and then it turns dusky. I like the way the land looks in that light. In summer it stays light, even at night. My climate is part of who I am.

Bouctouche: My Climate Report

Season	Average Temperature (how hot or cold it usually is)	Average Precipitation (the usual amount of snow and rain)
Winter (January)	−8°C	109 millimetres
Spring (April)	4°C	90 millimetres
Summer (July)	19°C	100 millimetres
Fall (October)	8°C	100 millimetres

Notes:

Our climate isn't too hot or too cold. We get a lot of snow and freezing rain in winter, and quite a bit of rain in summer and fall. That's part of living on a coast. What I like best are the fresh ocean breezes and windy days that make the waves high.

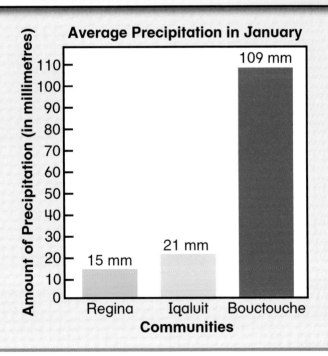

Average Precipitation in January

1. **How are the climates of the three communities different?**

2. **How would you describe the climate of your community? Where could you find this information?**

How Did Our Communities Start?

Have you ever wondered why communities started where they did? Linda, Meeka, and Michel will explain how physical geography (land, water, and climate) played a part in the beginnings of their communities.

Why People First Lived in the Regina Area

It had many bison. The first people here, the Blackfoot, the Plains Cree, the Saulteaux, and the Assiniboine, used bison for food, clothing, and shelter.

The Canadian Pacific Railway and a train station were built in the area. After that, many people came to settle.

REGINA **AREA**

The climate meant that there was enough rainfall for growing crops.

It had a creek that supplied water for drinking.

The flat land and rich soil were good for farming and ranching.

Why People First Lived in the Iqaluit Area

It had rivers and lakes that supplied water for drinking.

The rivers and bays meant people could travel by boat.

IQALUIT

AREA

The waters had many fish and seals, used by the Inuit for food and clothing.

Many caribou lived on the land. The Inuit used the caribou for food and clothing.

Why People First Lived in the Bouctouche Area

There were many fish to eat.

The climate was mild.

BOUCTOUCHE

AREA

The first people here, the Mi'kmaq, used the many trees to build their homes and canoes.

The calm waters were good for fishing and travelling by boat. The rivers supplied water for drinking.

There were many animals. The Mi'kmaq used the animal skins for clothing.

The land was fairly flat and the soil was rich, which was good for farming.

How does geography play a part in a community getting started?

Identity and Geography

Identity means who you are. When people are citizens of a community, they share an identity. Read what Linda, Meeka, and Michel say about the identity they share with their community.

Our citizens are proud to live in Regina. We feel a connection to our Prairie farmlands and to our big sky. We like our sunshine. We like our lake and parks. All these things help shape our identity, or who we are.

Many things about Iqaluit's geography make us who we are. We are Inuit from the Arctic. We are tied to the cold and the rocky, frozen land. We are coastal people, and we feel a connection to our ocean and rivers.

NEL

People in Bouctouche feel a connection to our waters. We are proud of our long sand dune and our bay. Acadians are proud to live on Canada's East Coast. All these things help make us who we are.

1. **How does the physical geography of your community shape your identity? That means, how does the land, water, and climate affect who you are?**

2. **What part of your community's physical geography would you miss most if you had to leave?**

Daily Life in Our Communities

What is daily life like for Linda, Meeka, and Michel? To find out, read these pages from their journals.

January 18

I woke up at 8 a.m. It was dark. I heard Dad shovelling our driveway. We had cereal and juice for breakfast. We listened to the news on CBC Radio. There will be more sunshine today!

Mom drove me to school. In Music we pretended we were in a band. Then Mrs. Oleski told us about the planets.

After school Dad and I made a snow fort. I like our clear, sunny days. I helped him make pizza for supper. I watched cartoons while it baked.

Then I had gymnastics. I like the balance beam. Mom went to her course at the university. We drove by Wascana Lake on the way home. The legislative building looks pretty at night, all lit up. I like the way the lights shine on the lake.

Time for bed. I can hear a bus drive by. Saturday we're going to my uncle's farm not far from Regina. I like seeing the flat prairie, but I like the city too.

January 18

When I woke up, I could hear CBC Radio North. I could also hear the wind howling. I knew I would need my sealskin mitts and kamiit instead of my other mitts and boots.

I had cocoa and pilot biscuits with jam for breakfast. Dad walked me to school. The roads are slippery and there are a lot of snowmobiles and big trucks. We have to be careful.

Daylight was breaking when I got to school. I had Inuktitut lessons in the morning. At recess we slid on the packed snow. For lunch I went home for some of Grandmother's soup. On my way back the sun was already setting.

After school we slid on the hill. We watched planes land at the airport. I want to be a pilot when I grow up. For supper at Grandmother's we had my favourite— caribou. I can use my own ulu to cut it now. I give the nicest pieces to Grandmother, the way Mom taught me.

My friends and I went skating at the arena tonight. Then I did homework and watched TV. Now it's bedtime. The wind is calmer. I can hear the sled dogs howling. I always think they're singing goodnight to one another.

January 18

Mom woke me up at 7 a.m. It was dark. She made eggs, ham, and toast for us. Then my sister and I put on our snowsuits, boots, hats, and mittens and waited for the school bus. It was cold! I waved to M. Gallant. He walks along the bay every morning. He says he loves the salty air. I do too.

In Language Arts class we wrote about our favourite animals. Then we had Music. A lady sang some very old Acadian songs for us.

After school Mom took us down to the river to watch people fish for smelt. The river is frozen, and there are little cabins all over the ice. They look like little villages.

For supper we had fricot and homemade bread. Then I had hockey practice. When we drove home, the town was quiet. The snow banks are over a metre tall. They squeak when you walk on them! CBC Radio-Canada said we'll get more snow tomorrow. Time for bed now.

Some things about our lives are the same. We have families and schools. We all like to play. Some of our differences are because Canada is so big. We live far from one another, but there are ways we can connect. We have telephones and the Internet. We can take an airplane to visit one another. We learn about one another at school. We learn about other communities by reading, watching television shows, and hearing the news on the radio.

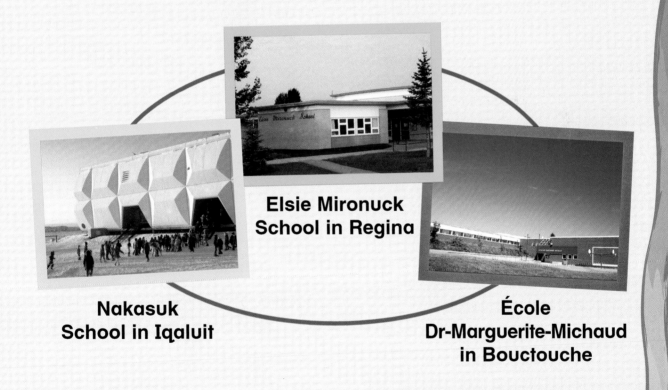

Elsie Mironuck
School in Regina

Nakasuk
School in Iqaluit

École
Dr-Marguerite-Michaud
in Bouctouche

1. How are the lives of Linda, Meeka, and Michel the same? How are their lives different?

2. What is your daily life like?

About Our Cultures: Language

If you visit, you'll see that our stop signs are in English. Most people in Regina speak English. People in the Francophone community speak French. Other languages are also spoken, because Regina has people from many cultures.

In Iqaluit our stop signs are in Inuktitut and in English. Inuktitut is spoken by most people in Iqaluit. Many people also speak English and some speak French. People who have moved here from other countries also speak their first language.

Here in Bouctouche our stop signs are in the two official languages of Canada: English and French. Most people here speak French. People who have moved here from other countries also speak their first language.

1. **What language do most people in your community speak?**

2. **Name some of the other languages people in your community speak.**

About Our Cultures: Places and Symbols

Every community has places and things that make it special. Pictures of the special things are called symbols. Places and symbols help shape our identity as people of a community.

Community	Coat of Arms	Flag
Regina	The coat of arms of Regina	The flag of Regina
Iqaluit	The coat of arms of Nunavut	The flag of Nunavut
Bouctouche	The coat of arms of Bouctouche	The flag of Acadia

1. If someone visited your community, what would you take the person to see? How do those places or things show your community's identity?

2. Why are special places and symbols important to the people in a community?

Place	Logo	Symbol
Our legislative building	Logo for our Saskatchewan Roughriders	Sign for our RCMP buildings
Our airport	Iqaluit Logo for our city	An inuksuk, an Inuit symbol
Our Acadian village: Le Pays de la Sagouine	LE PAYS DE LA SAGOUINE Logo for Le Pays de la Sagouine	Sign for our dune

About Our Cultures: Traditions and Celebrations

A tradition is doing or believing something the same way that a certain group of people does. A celebration is a way to be happy or proud about something.

Some performers from our Mosaic Festival

Regina's Mosaic Festival celebrates the many cultures of our city through music, dancing, and arts. We have agricultural shows because farming is important to us. We have Buffalo Days, with a rodeo and parade. It helps us remember the people who first lived here: the First Nations, Métis, and early settlers. We celebrate being from the Prairies and Western Canada. Our Francophone citizens celebrate every year at La Fête fransaskoise.

In Iqaluit we stay close to our past, to our land, and to our Inuit culture. We keep many old traditions. Iqaluit has an Elders' Qammak, a small hut where the Inuit Elders teach our culture.

We celebrate special days with contests, songs, drumming...and food! At Toonik Tyme we celebrate spring and remember the people who were here long ago. We have dogsled racing, iglu building, and other contests. On Nunavut Day we celebrate the day our territory was created. We have an Arctic Food Celebration every year.

Toonik Tyme

In Bouctouche we celebrate being Acadian. We also celebrate being part of Eastern Canada and being close to the ocean. La Fête nationale de l'Acadie is our big Acadian festival. We have a tintamarre, a very noisy parade. There is music and food. We also have le Festival des mollusques. It has a parade, games...and lots of seafood!

We remember our first people, the Mi'kmaq. The Tjipogtotjg First Nation has a powwow every year to celebrate Mi'kmaq culture.

La Fête nationale de l'Acadie

A Community's Stories

Linda's class is making a book of stories told by people who have lived in her community for a long time. Linda's grandmother tells her this story.

When I was a girl, one day my grandfather and I walked into his fields. We made our way along the rows of wheat until our farmhouse looked small in the distance. Then he knelt and scooped some soil into his hand. He asked me what it was and I proudly gave him my answer: "Dirt!" He shook his head and said he was holding precious jewels. Then he took out his handkerchief and unwrapped a locket. He opened it and placed some of the dirt inside. Then he snapped it shut and gave it to me. I didn't understand. I didn't want a locket full of dirt!

On our way back to the house, he told me of his life on the farm. He told me of thunderstorms so strong they rattled the dishes, of winds so strong they blew out the windows. He told me of years so dry the soil and seed were carried away by the winds. He told me of good years when crops grew tall.

When I grew older, I understood why the land is so important. People in our community feel that the Prairie is part of who we are. Now I want you to have this locket to help you remember that.

1. **How does your community celebrate its past? How does it celebrate its cultures?**

2. **Why do celebrations, stories, and traditions strengthen people's ties to their community?**

Who Helped to Develop Our Communities?

The first people here were Plains Cree, Saulteaux, Assiniboine, and Blackfoot. In the Regina area the Plains Cree stacked bison bones in circles. They called it Oskana-Ka-asateki. French, British, and Métis

A train station in Regina, 1891

people came. Then many settlers came from Europe. Now we have people from many countries.

An Inuk Elder lights a qulliq (oil lamp) at a graduation.

The Inuit have always lived here. Other people came to hunt and fish. They called the area Frobisher Bay. Later it became an army centre. We changed back to our Inuktitut name, Iqaluit. It means Place of Many Fish. Most people here are Inuit, but we have people from many other places.

A Mi'kmaq Elder teaching the traditional art of making baskets

The Mi'kmaq were the first people here. They called the area Chebooktoosk. It means Great Little Harbour. Then French-speaking people came to the East Coast to fish and farm. They called the land Acadia. The Acadians were forced to leave because of a war between France and England. When they later came back, some came to our area. In our town we are mainly Francophone.

How is the past of each of these communities alike? How is it different?

How Are Our Communities Connected?

Our communities, Regina, Iqaluit, and Bouctouche, all began with Aboriginal peoples.

We all share our two official languages: French and English.

We connect through sports, music, stories, and arts.

We share holidays like Canada Day.

Our communities all have many cultures.

Our communities and citizens all have an identity.

Canada is a big country. Our communities are far apart. We have differences and we have things that are alike. We have many cultures and languages. Together as citizens we give Canada its identity.

I am from an Inuit community.

I am from an Acadian community.

I am from a Prairie community.

We are all Canadian.

1. **How is your community connected to other communities?**

2. **How is your community connected to Canada?**

Our Natural Resources

Natural resources are things we use from nature. Soil, trees, and water are some natural resources.

The most important natural resource in Regina is the land. The flat land and rich soil make good farmland. Other natural resources are oil and natural gas.

Iqaluit's most important natural resource is water. From the ocean, we get fish, seals, and walrus. Inuit rely on the land and sea for most of our traditional food, clothing, and art.

Water is the most important natural resource in Bouctouche. We use the waters for fishing. We also have our big sand dune that scientists study and tourists visit. The land around our city is good for farming. We live close to forests. Forests are a natural resource that gives us wood.

What are the natural resources in your community?

Work in Our Communities

Regina has many kinds of work. Because it is the capital of our province, many people work for the government. Many people work at jobs that help farmers. We have places for making steel pipe, fertilizer, and gas. These are some of our industries.

Making steel

An Inuk artist

Iqaluit is the capital of Nunavut. Many people work in government jobs. Some work in the transportation industry. They drive trucks, boats, and taxis, or work at the airport. Some people have jobs that help tourists. Many Inuit are artists.

Actors and tourists at Le Pays de la Sagouine

Fishing is one industry in Bouctouche. Some people work at a big place that packs seafood. Some work at a place that builds parts for houses. Many people work at the tourist sites. There are many kinds of jobs and industries in my town.

What are some jobs in your community?

Goods and Services in Our Communities

Goods

Goods are things that are made and that we can buy.

Services

A service is a type of work that helps people or gives them something they need. Some services we pay for.

In Regina we have many stores for the goods we need, such as food and clothes. We have services such as banks and schools. One of our special services is fixing farm machinery.

In Iqaluit we have stores for the goods we need. Many of our goods come from far away. We have services such as an airport and a library. One special service is providing tours of the Arctic.

In Bouctouche we have stores for the goods we need. We have services such as parks, an arena, and a wharf for boats. A special service is offering places for tourists to stay.

1. **What is a store in your community that sells goods?**

2. **What is a place in your community that gives a service?**

How Industry Can Affect Our Communities

uses these
natural resources:
- rich soil
- flat land
- water for crops
  and animals

provides jobs like these:
- farming (growing crops for food)
- ranching (raising animals)

The Farming Industry

needs other jobs and services
like these:
- running of grain elevators
- animal sales
- farm machinery sales
  and repairs
- veterinarian services

helps shape a community's
identity as a farming
community

can cause disagreement
about land use

uses these natural resources:
- land for oil and natural gas
- land and rocks for minerals
- waters for fish and seafood
- forests for lumber

provides jobs like these:
- jobs in factories
- jobs in transportation (loading and trucking the goods)

The Manufacturing Industry
(the making of goods)

needs other jobs and services like these:
- machinery repair
- building of the factories
- housing for the workers and their families
- schools and stores for the workers and families

helps shape a community's identity as a manufacturing community

can cause disagreement about
- land use
- environmental problems (pollution)

What would happen if one of the industries in your community had to shut down?

The Characteristics of My Community

You have learned about the characteristics of three Canadian communities. Now it's time to learn about your own community.

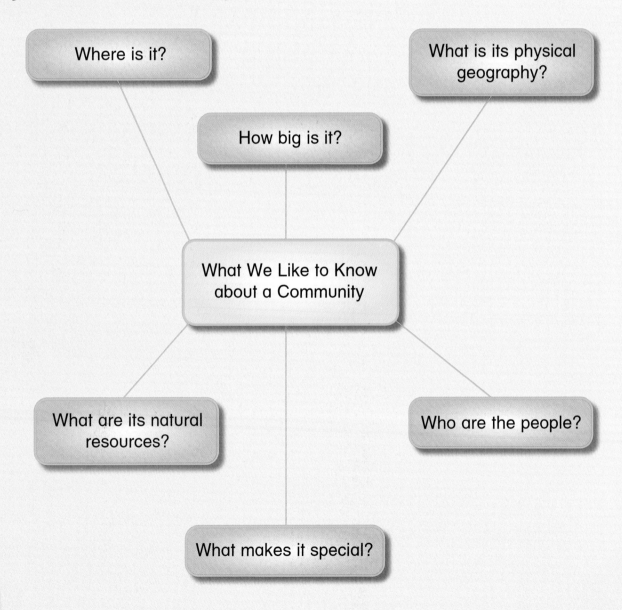

Where is it?

What is its physical geography?

How big is it?

What We Like to Know about a Community

What are its natural resources?

Who are the people?

What makes it special?

What Makes My Community Special?

Every community has things that make it special. The people who live there make it special. The community's name and the story of how the community got started are special. Communities in Canada share many things that are alike, but they all have something special that gives them their own identity.

Alberta communities have many special characteristics.

Drumheller is in the Alberta Badlands. The area has many dinosaur bones. It has one of the biggest dinosaur museums in the world!

The community of **Lac La Biche** started in 1798 as a fur-trading post. It was started by David Thompson, who was an explorer and mapmaker. The first members of the community were Métis people. Métis were children of First Nations people who married fur traders and settlers, many of them French. In 1853 Father Remas started a large French mission at Lac La Biche.

Fort Macleod is a place to learn about history. The town has a fort just like the one that was there long ago. The museum there shows the history of the fort and of the Blackfoot who used to camp in that area.

Fort Chipewyan is in an area known for its wildlife. It has over 200 kinds of birds. Nearby Wood Buffalo National Park has a herd of wild bison that roams free on the land.

1. Use a map of Alberta to find these places. Is your community near or far from these places?

2. What makes your community special?

How Did My Community Start?

All communities have a beginning. How did communities begin long ago?

The first people in Canada were Aboriginal peoples. They lived in many different groups across the country. Alberta's First Nations lived in many regions. Some lived in the forests. Some lived on the grassy plains. Each group had its own language, traditions, and beliefs.

Today, First Nations continue to have communities throughout the province.

These pictures carved in rock were found in Writing-on-Stone Provincial Park. They are called petroglyphs. Aboriginal peoples carved them about 100 to 3500 years ago.

Long ago, people came to our area from Eastern Canada and from other countries. Fur traders and explorers came. Many were from Quebec and were of French heritage. Many were Métis. Many were of British heritage. They built forts and trading posts. Some people came to build churches and missions. Then settlers came to build homes and farms. Later, people came to Canada from all over the world. All these people helped to start communities.

Early communities usually had a main street like this.

Why Did People Come Here?

How did people choose where to settle? First Nations peoples knew all about the land, waterways, and climate, so they could choose good places to live. They knew where to hunt and where to find other kinds of food. The explorers and fur traders learned from them and used trails that they had made.

A Woodlands Cree tipi, 1882

Communities often started near rivers or lakes. People could travel on them by boat. They also needed the water for drinking and washing. When the railway was built, some communities started near the train stations. Some communities started where the land was good for farming.

Canadian Pacific Railway train in Calgary, 1884

How could you find out about how your community began?

Who Helped to Develop My Community?

Long ago, First Nations had Chiefs and Elders who helped develop their communities. They helped their communities survive and grow.

First Nations helped other communities develop too. Long ago in our area when settlers started communities, First Nations peoples showed the newcomers ways to live on the land. They guided explorers like David Thompson who made maps of the land.

French people started many communities in Canada. The first European language spoken in our area was French. Leaders like Father Lacombe and Bishop Grandin set up missions.

Francophone settlers at Sylvan Lake in 1904

The Métis helped many communities in Canada grow. They started settlements and helped newcomers learn about the land.

People came to Canada from all over the world. They built roads and railways. They mined. They built houses and stores. They farmed and ranched.

All these people helped communities grow.

A Métis family in 1900

What groups of people helped your community grow?

How My Community Has Changed

How Transportation Has Changed

Long ago, there were no cars. In our area First Nations peoples walked from place to place. When the Blackfoot brought horses to the area, many First Nations used the horses for riding and for pulling loads. First Nations who lived near water used canoes.

A travois helped carry loads, 1887.

A wagon and team of oxen, 1900

Settlers of long ago rode and carried goods in wagons that were pulled by horses or oxen.

Settlers also travelled by steamboat and by steam-powered trains.

A steamboat leaving Edmonton, 1896

Now we have many different kinds of transportation. We have cars, trucks, buses, and airplanes. We drive on paved roads and highways.

A busy highway of today

How Schools Have Changed

Long ago, schools only had one room and one teacher. The teacher taught all the grades. There was no electricity long ago, so wood stoves were used for heat. Students had to carry in the wood for the stove. Children had to walk or ride a horse to school, and it was often a long way. The schools were plain and not very comfortable. There were few supplies like paper or pencils.

The first school in Bon Accord, 1904

Now schools are bigger. They have many teachers and classrooms. Some students ride buses or get car rides to school. Schools have electricity and are comfortable. They have many kinds of supplies.

École Oriole Park Elementary, Red Deer

How Homes Have Changed

Long ago, some First Nations, such as the Blackfoot, Stoney, and Plains Cree, lived in tipis.

A Blackfoot tipi

Long ago, some settlers lived in houses made of sod. When they arrived, they needed shelter right away. If an area had no trees for making logs for a house, they used squares of sod cut from the ground. Later, when they could get logs, they would build a log house.

A sod house

Now people live in apartment buildings and houses. We have many kinds of homes in our communities.

Houses of today

1. **What is something else that has changed from long ago?**

2. **Who could you ask to find out more about things that have changed?**

Why Has My Community Changed?

Communities change when there are changes to the land. Maybe a mall is built on land that was a grassy field. Maybe a playground is built where a parking lot used to be.

Communities change when buildings go up. They change when buildings come down. They change when new stores open. They change when stores close. They change when new industries start and when industries stop.

Communities change when new people arrive. People bring their own traditions and cultures. Some people bring their own language. The community changes and grows as the cultures of the citizens mix.

Communities change when people move away. Sometimes people have to move because they can't find work in the community. Some people have to move because they need more services than their community offers.

1. **What changes have you noticed in your community?**

2. **How do changes to a community affect its identity?**

The People in My Community

How Have the People Changed?

Communities change over the years for many reasons. Maybe they began long ago with just a few people or families. As more people came from other parts of Canada and from many countries, communities gained more cultures and languages.

These community members celebrate their Ukrainian culture.

Communities are linked to their jobs and industries. If those change, the community changes too. A mining community whose mines shut down would have to change to a different industry so that there would be jobs for the people.

Communities change when they change in size. They can change in other ways too.

A community changes when new citizens bring their cultures, traditions, and languages.

A community changes when the age of its citizens changes.

How Have We Stayed the Same?

Our communities have changed over the years, but we always remember the people who started them.

We remember the First Nations who were the first people here. Today, there are 44 First Nations bands in Alberta, who keep their cultures and traditions strong.

We now have a National Aboriginal Day.

Statue of Father Lacombe in St. Albert

We remember the French-speaking people who helped start many communities. Today, Alberta has a strong Francophone community. We have Francophone schools. We have schools for learning to speak French as a second language, because it is one of Canada's two official languages.

It is easy to see our past. We have celebrations of our past. We learn about our past and our cultures at school. We learn our languages there too. We learn from our Elders and family members. Our communities have statues and museums to help us learn our history.

Keeping links to our past, languages, and cultures helps us build our identity.

A Chinese New Year celebration in Edmonton

1. **How do we see our First Nations and Francophone heritage in our communities today?**

2. **How can we show respect to all the people in our community?**

People Who Change a Community

Everywhere in Canada there are people who help make their community better.

Some people help by welcoming new people to the community.

Some people join clubs that help the community.

Helping at a food bank

Helping a neighbour

Some people help by cleaning up garbage on the streets.

Some people help by visiting seniors.

Some people help by taking part in celebrations.

Ruth Kidder is from Peace River. She serves as the President of the Alberta Aboriginal Women's Society. She is also part of Métis organizations. Ruth is legally blind. She takes pride in her culture and works to help keep it strong.

Debbie Lam lives in Calgary. She won an Alberta's Great Kids Award in 2003 when she was 11. In her school's Leadership Club she helped younger students with the breakfast program, buddy reading, computers, and gym. She is helpful and takes responsibility.

Max Gurela is from Millet. He won an Alberta's Great Kids Award in 2003 when he was six. He played a role in protecting his community's environment. He had a compost bin set up at his school and he made a plan for paper recycling.

Joël Cadrin, 17, and Andre Lambert, 16, are from Edmonton. They and other members of their St-Thomas d'Aquin youth group help Francophone people who have moved to the city. They help collect items that the newcomers may need for their homes.

1. Do you know someone who helps your community?

2. What does your community need help with?

Being Part of a Community

Meeka, Michel, and Linda have come back to say goodbye. First they told you about their communities. They explained how a community's physical geography helps shape its identity. They showed how communities are both different and alike.

Then you learned about communities in Alberta. You learned how they started and who helped them develop. You learned how they change. You learned how people help their community.

Our Canadian communities are all connected. They are places to be proud of. You are part of a community. Being part of a community helps you know who you are.

1. **What makes you proud of your community?**

2. **What do you like about being part of your community?**